THE SENSORY COMPOUNDING WORKBOOK

Using your five senses to create inner peace and calm

APRIL NELSON

BALBOA.PRESS

A DIVISION OF HAY HOUSE

Balboa Press books may be ordered through booksellers or by contacting:

Balboa Press
A Division of Hay House
1663 Liberty Drive
Bloomington, IN 47403
www.balboapress.com
1 (877) 407-4847

Because of the dynamic nature of the Internet, any web addresses or links contained in
this book may have changed since publication and may no longer be valid. The views
expressed in this work are solely those of the author and do not necessarily reflect the views
of the publisher, and the publisher hereby disclaims any responsibility for them.

The author of this book does not dispense medical advice or prescribe the use of any technique as a form
of treatment for physical, emotional, or medical problems without the advice of a physician, either directly
or indirectly. The intent of the author is only to offer information of a general nature to help you in your quest
for emotional and spiritual well-being. In the event you use any of the information in this book for yourself,
which is your constitutional right, the author and the publisher assume no responsibility for your actions.

ISBN: 978-1-9822-4216-9 (sc)
ISBN: 978-1-9822-4217-6 (e)

Library of Congress Control Number: 2020901759

Print information available on the last page.

Balboa Press rev. date: 02/07/2020

Contents

For permission requests, contact the publisher at:
Sensorybound Counseling, Inc.
www.sensoryboundcounselling.com

Thank you to Donna Kerr from Kerr Creative Inc. for all her help in making this workbook possible.

Ordering Information:
Quantity sales. Special discounts are available on quantity purchases by corporations, associations, and others. For details, contact the publisher at the address above.

Welcome

Welcome to the Sensory Compounding Workbook! You will learn about all five of your senses and how to use them to create a safe, peaceful and relaxed state.

How can it help?

Sensory Compounding teaches you to become more aware and intentional about your senses and to use all five senses together to create inner peace and calm—anywhere, anytime. This sense-ability can help you reprogram old, unhelpful reactions and create new helpful, relaxing reactions to sensory information.

Where did it come from?

The beginnings of Sensory Compounding began when its creator, April Nelson, was looking for a way to find some peace following the passing of her mother. She began going to regular massage therapy sessions. Her massage therapist always had the same aroma in the massage room and April began to associate this smell with relaxing her muscles (that noodle feeling). One day she had to wait in the waiting room where she could still smell her, by now, favourite aroma. She noticed that her muscles relaxed all on their own, without the massage.

This is what's called conditioning and it's what you'll learn to do in Sensory Compounding.

As a Therapist, April had had training in conditioning but it had never connected until that day in the waiting room. She began to explore the possibility of using conditioning as a way to address something that she saw frequently in her therapy practice.

April had observed that so much of therapy is "in the head," processing thinking and feelings, but so much of life experience is stored in the physical body. It manifests as stress, tightness, agitation, etc. and she saw it frequently in her clients. The "head" types of therapies did not seem as effective in helping clients learn what was happening in their bodies, let alone do something about it.

April wondered how these two very important concepts could be integrated on a deeper level to create a more complete experience for each person.

    ⓘ A common experience of trauma is that the mind and body become disconnected. The "mind" methods work to connect to the mind so people can become more present in their lives. The issue is how to connect to the body which is carrying its own set of symptoms. The senses are the way the body interacts with the world. It makes sense to access the body through the senses!

April began to use conditioning with clients, pairing mindfulness meditation with sensory cues (aromas, at first) that taught clients to reach a safe, relaxing, peaceful place. With further research, she added *compounding*, which means using more than one sense as the cues. If one sense (aroma) worked, it made sense that adding more sensory cues would work even better.

It developed into Sensory Compounding which is what you're learning in this workbook. Her clients began to tell her that they were feeling better, were calmer and more relaxed, and could manage stressful situations better.

Her dream of an accessible, affordable way of reaching a peaceful, relaxed physical state had come true.

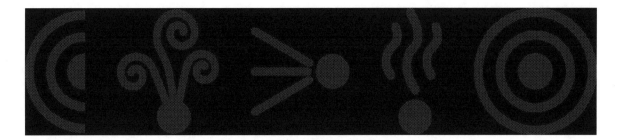

The five senses

Your senses connect you to the world. Each sense organ takes in physical information from the environment and then sends signals to the brain for processing. How all this works is complex and there is a lot that is not yet known. We won't get into intense anatomy, physiology, chemistry and all the other sciences that help us understand how our senses work. We don't need to. What we need to know to create our own sense-ability is two main ideas.

Senses are physical

The first is that senses are physical. In other words, the smells, sights, sounds, touches and tastes that we take in are actual physical things like vibrations, light waves and chemicals. These physical senses developed to serve a function—to warn us, let us know what might be good or bad to eat, and many others that we'll learn.

Senses are more than physical

The second idea is that sensory information also involves emotion, memory and thinking. The brain takes the sense signals and processes them in some really complex ways. We might have a strong memory of past holidays when we smell turkey. A certain color might make us feel happy. The sound of thunder might trigger a memory from childhood as well as make us feel afraid. These associations are what we're working with here. They can change over time. The same physical sensation (such as a sight or a smell) can be experienced differently at different times.

Senses work together

We will look at each sense by itself in the following pages, but in reality, our senses work together (this is compounding at its finest!). For example, if you are asked to imagine the smell of an object, you will picture that object in your mind. Researchers have found that the brain's visual center lights up with activity when someone does a purely smell-related task.

Another example is eating. It involves all 5 senses: taste, smell, touch, hearing and sight. You can't just shut one off. And each sense adds its own magic to the experience and the combined result is a rich experience.

When we involve all 5 senses, we can create more powerful experiences. We will be doing "multi-sensory design."

Try it out
Imagine the smell of an orange. You can't help but picture an orange in your mind.

Hearing

As you go through your day, you hear many things, good and not-so-good:

A.M. The alarm clock's insistent beep wakes you up and you can hear traffic sounds through your open window. Rush hour is starting. The sound of your coffee maker finishing its brew steers you to the kitchen. You love the sound of the coffee as you pour it into your favourite mug. As you wait for the bus, the noise of the street annoys you as it always does. When you get to work, you feel your body come on alert when you hear the sounds of voices, keyboards and ringing phones.

P.M. You go to lunch at a crowded café that's so noisy you can hardly hear your lunch companions. It leaves you tired from the strain of trying to hear them. Back at work, the non-stop ringing of your phone leaves you wanting to throw it through a window. On the bus ride home, you put in your earplugs and listen to some soothing music to relax. Later that night, you have fun dancing at a club to the cranked up tunes. When you get home, your ears are still ringing.

4 sounds

Before we move on to learn about your sense of hearing, take a few minutes to think about it. Write or draw four sounds you can hear (if you can't identify four, write as many as you can):

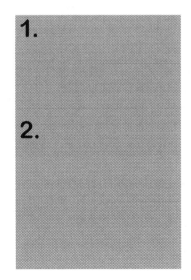

1.

2.

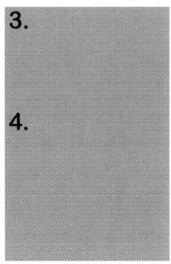

3.

4.

What is hearing?

Put very simply, hearing is good (and not-so-good) vibrations. When we listen to the Beach Boys song "Good Vibrations," we are actually hearing vibrations. The ears do an amazing job of processing vibrations into what we call sounds.

The outer ear with all its curls and wiggles actually channels the vibrations into the ear canal. The vibrations then strike the ear drums (just like a real drum) and then move on to the inner ear where tiny hairs convert the vibrations to electrical signals that are sent to the brain. And that's the really simple explanation!

Why do we have hearing?

We are always hearing something. In fact, pure silence may not be good for us.

ⓘ Complete silence is impossible, and even not beneficial. There are some chambers designed to dampen and absorb sound— as close as we can get to complete silence. In such a quiet location, what happens is that one starts hearing their own heart, and even the flowing of the blood as it passes through our head, or the high pitched sound that our ear produces when things get quiet. Even our breathing becomes a unique acoustic phenomena that draws our attention. People might also experience some disorientation, dizziness and even euphoric feeling.[1]

Hearing helps keep you safe

Hearing operates in all directions and alerts us to things in the environment. We are especially tuned to catch new or different sounds as they can signal danger or alert us to "pay attention." Hikers in areas with dangerous animals learn that sudden silence is not a good thing. We will often be woken up into full awareness by an unfamiliar sound. For example, we sleep through the TV, but wake up to the sound of glass breaking.

Hearing allows us to locate where sounds are coming from (so we know which way to run). Sound arrives at your ears at different times (measured in millionths of a second) depending on the direction it's coming from. A sound to your right arrives at your right ear a tiny bit before it arrives at your left ear. Your head also gets in the way of the sound reaching your left ear, adding a slight delay. This is why we move our heads to locate where a sound is coming from.

Hearing is relational

The design of our ears enhances the frequencies of human speech. The importance of hearing other people seems to be built-in to the ears. Hearing speech is the foundation of interacting with other people. You become aware of that if you travel to a country where you cannot speak the language. It's pretty isolating!

> It's not just the words we use, but also the intonation and rhythm that our hearing picks up, detecting the subtleties and nuances in speech that enable us to know whether someone is lying, or sad, or tired, or nervous or excited or any other state they might be in.[2]

These non-verbal sounds are essential to communication and are missing in written communication. It's why e-mails can result in major conflicts (called flame wars) when people misinterpret the nuances of written words. Do you use emoticons when you're texting? They are an attempt to fill in some of the missing information we can hear if the person was speaking.

> The problems of deafness are deeper and more complex, if not more important, than those of blindness. Deafness is a much worse misfortune. For it means the loss of the most vital stimulus—the sound of the voice that brings language, sets thoughts astir and keeps us in the intellectual company of man.
>
> Helen Keller

Hearing and emotion

Our hearing feeds directly into our emotions. Sounds can soothe and calm us or annoy and stress us. Music can trigger all kinds of emotions. Movie and TV music greatly influences the emotions you feel while watching. All kinds of other sounds can be soothing or annoying and it depends on the person. One person might find the sound of wind soothing, while another person might feel anxious.

My preferences

Everyone has sound preferences. What are yours?

Sounds that soothe and relax you

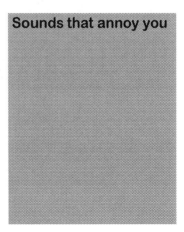

Sounds that annoy you

Keeping your balance

One more function of the ears is that they contribute to balance. If you've ever had an ear infection, you might have lost your ability to balance. The ear has special canals that are filled with fluid. The fluid moves when your head moves and sends messages to the brain about how and where your body is moving.

Now hear this - fun facts

- WorkSafe BC found that 25% of young people entering the workforce had early warning signs of hearing loss, with a further 4.6% showing "abnormal" results on hearing tests. [18]
- A leading cause of hearing loss is exposure to excessively loud sounds (90 decibels or higher). Construction equipment, sirens, loud music at concerts/clubs and listening through earphones at high volume can all cause hearing damage.
- When you go up to high elevations, the change in pressure causes your ears to pop.
- Some animals have different hearing organs. Snakes hear through their jawbones and male mosquitoes hear through their antennae.
- Bats and whales can send out sound waves that bounce off objects. They can then "read" the echoes to locate objects (this is called echolocation). Turns out humans can do it too. Some blind people have developed a form of echolocation using sounds and clicks. They use their hearing to navigate.
- Car makers spend a lot of time and money on the sounds a car makes. One sound that gets a lot of attention is the sound of the door closing. Many of the top automobile brands have door development teams, with design engineers dedicated to fine-tuning their particular—signature—door-closing sound. [19]

Hearing sense-ability

Here are some activities to get to know your sense of hearing.

Good/ not-so-good things

Every sense has some things you will like about it and some you won't. Write them out here.

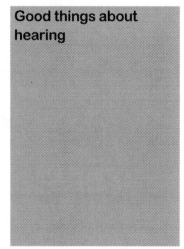

Good things about hearing

Not-so-good things

How important is it?

On a scale of 1 to 10, how important is your sense of hearing? Circle your answer.

1	2	3	4	5	6	7	8	9	10

Not important   Important

(?) **What makes it important (or not)?**

....
....
....
....
....

One day

Choose one day in the near future when you will be "sound aware."
Simply be aware of what you are hearing during the day. If you'd like, cut
out this form and carry it with you for the day.

Time	What am I hearing?	How does it affect me?

Watch with no sound

Watch a movie or TV show with the sound turned off. Note your
reactions to the program. What is it like to not be able to hear the
dialogue? Do you get caught up in the drama without the music?

Practice

With practice, your hearing center in the brain gets
better at detecting different sounds. With training,
piano tuners and musicians can tune by ear, music
lovers can pick out notes that others can't hear, and
social scientists can predict if a couple will break up
by what they hear them saying (and the tone of voice
while saying it).

What sounds would you like to get better at hearing?

Taste

As you go through your day, you taste many things, good and sometimes not-so-good:

A.M. The wonderful taste of your first cup of coffee (or other beverage). You try a few candies someone left out at work, but you don't like their sourness so you spit them out. You go for an early lunch at a bakery café and nearly swoon at the taste of freshly baked bread and butter. The savoury soup is a wonderful complement and you're delighted with your lunch.

P.M. The orange you eat for an afternoon pick-me-up has a tangy bite that reminds you of summer days. Dinner was so-so as you tried a new frozen pizza and didn't like it very much. You drink a glass of milk for an evening snack and grimace with distaste. You're trying to get more calcium, but you really don't like milk. The refreshing mint flavour of your toothpaste removes the milk residue and you head off for bed.

4 tastes

Before we move on to learn about your sense of taste, take a few minutes to think about taste. Write or draw four tastes you have experienced today (if you can't identify four tastes, write as many as you can):

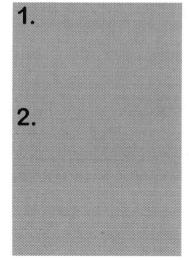

1.

2.

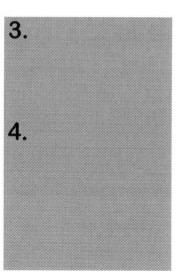

3.

4.

Taste needs action

Taste is the only sense that is tied to an action. We cannot taste without putting something in our mouths where the taste receptors are located.

That's why the "4 Tastes" exercise above is the only time you have to think in the past about what you sensed (unless you're eating or drinking while reading this!).

Taste and smell go together

It might seem as though you can taste things in the air, but you're really smelling them. Taste and smell go together like bread and butter. Some researchers estimate that over 80% of "taste" is actually smell. Have you ever had a bad head cold and found you couldn't taste food at all, or it didn't taste right? That's because your sense of smell was blocked by your stuffy nose.

ⓘ Astronauts tend to lose their sense of smell since reduced gravity in space leads to stuffy noses. So they use lots of condiments to jazz up the flavour of food.

What is taste?

When we talk about taste, we are actually talking about flavour. Flavour has a simple formula:

Smell + taste = flavour

And there's a lot more than taste and smell going on when you eat! There's texture, physical temperature, perceived temperature ("coolness" such as menthol and spicy "hotness") and sound. All of the senses are involved in eating!

ⓘ In a study on potato chips, it was found that perception of crispness and staleness were altered by varying the loudness or pitch of the "crunching" noise. When the sound of crunching was amplified, participants rated the chips as both crispier and fresher.[3]

Why do we have taste?

Taste helps us identify harmful foods and foods that are okay to eat. All basic tastes are either appetitive (we want to eat them) or aversive (we want to avoid them). A bitter or sour taste was a sign of poisonous plants or rotting meat. Sweetness and saltiness often signal nutrient-rich foods. Taste tells you what to swallow and what to spit out.

Think of our early human ancestors in the jungle or on the savannah. In a world of grasses, leaves, insects, animals (alive or dead and decomposing), fruits, and dozens of other categories of potential food, they had no automatic knowledge of what was digestible, nutritious, or poisonous. Yet, they had to eat or die. Their vision and hearing, although essential for avoiding predators, were not much help in selecting food, but their sense of taste, combined with smell, provided a critical guide. Many poisonous or indigestible plants are bitter; fruit, with its high carbohydrate content for energy, is sweet; and salt, necessary for human survival, is appealing. Taste as a guide is not infallible, of course, but it is what evolution has provided to solve the problem of eating the right food.[4]

Our sense of taste gives us what the experts call nutritional wisdom. Non-experts call it craving. What we eat one day will affect what we crave the next day. If we eat a lot of sweet food one day, the next day we'll likely crave salt or savory food. We need a balance of carbohydrates and protein. Over time, the body learns to associate flavours with food that we need. When we're low on something we need, the body sends a signal through craving.[5] Of course, eating way too much of one type of food can throw this natural ability off.

(?) Have you noticed food cravings?

....

....

....

(?) Is there any pattern to them?

....

....

....

You could try to keep a record and it might show your nutritional wisdom.

How it works

Taste is the other chemical sense (as is smell). When we detect tastes, we are actually detecting chemicals. The bumps on your tongue contain many taste buds which have receptors that detect flavours. Taste buds are also located in the roof, sides, and back of the mouth with some more in the throat. The taste buds send signals to different parts of the brain where information from other senses (like temperature and smell) is added.

One of the brain's taste pathways is linked to the part of the brain that generates reflexes. We have reflex reactions to food such as licking our lips, moving our tongues and salivating (hence the term "mouth-watering"). There are also rejection reflexes, such as gagging and spitting out obnoxious food or drink. We can't control these behaviours, they're reflexes!

Types of taste

The sensation of taste can be categorized into five basic tastes: sweetness, sourness, saltiness, bitterness, and umami.

Sweetness

Sweetness is usually a pleasant taste (too pleasant if you're trying to cut back on sugar!). Sweet foods are high-energy and were essential to survival. Children have notorious sweet-tooths, which may be nature's way of helping them eat enough calories.

Sourness

Sourness is the taste that detects acidity. Sour is an aversive taste. Some researchers believe our reaction to sourness is built-in rather than learned. Newborns react to sourness before they can make learned associations.

> How much pleasure we take in sour tastes seems unusually malleable. Infants do reject sourness, but quite a few young children go through a phase when they prefer very sour tastes, and sour flavours are important components of many cuisines. [4]

Saltiness

Saltiness is a taste produced by sodium. It is a pleasurable taste. Our preference for salt is another taste that might be built-in rather than learned. Salt is necessary for survival but is often rare in natural diets. So we might be wired to load up on it when we can. This sure makes sticking to a low-salt diet difficult!

Bitterness

The most sensitive of the tastes, bitterness is usually experienced as unpleasant or aversive. Children are quite sensitive to bitterness which helps protect them from dangerous foods. You can develop a taste for bitter flavours like coffee, nicotine, bitter chocolate and hoppy beer.

Umami

Umami (or savory) was discovered in Japan and was slowly adopted as a flavour in the West. It is an appetitive taste and is a savory or meaty taste. Umami is a signal that the food is rich in protein.

Are there more tastes?

Researchers suspect there may be more tastes with specialized sensory cells. Leading candidates for new tastes include fat, alkaline, metallic and carbon dioxide.

(?) What are your taste preferences?

....
....
....
....

Changing tastes

Our tastes change over time. Some of this is pure biology. With age, we lose taste receptors on our tongue (by the age of 20, we've lost half our receptors). Children might be fussy eaters because they can taste more than adults. Many elderly people lose interest in foods they can no longer taste well. This can contribute to losing weight and poorer health. As with smell, the more you use your taste sense, the less you'll lose it. Changes in taste preferences are normal. When we're young, we tend to prefer sweet foods. As we get older, we often get more adventurous and try new tastes. We can develop different tastes over time. Culture and environment play a large role in developing tastes. Sometimes you might set out to develop a taste for something you didn't like. It's possible with practice.

(?) **How have your taste preferences changed over time?**

....
....
....
....

Taste and emotion

Because taste is combined with smell (which is wired to memory), our sense of taste is closely linked to our emotions. Certain tastes can evoke an emotional reaction. There are many phrases in English that express these pleasant and unpleasant taste-emotion reactions: bittersweet, a bitter pill, sour grapes, sweet nothings. One research study found that phrases that include a taste-emotion metaphor triggered both the taste and emotion centres in the brain.[6]

Tasty tidbits - fun facts

- Taste and taste sensations can be developed with some work. An example is the tolerance for hot chili peppers. People compete to develop the hottest chili in the world—the winner is in the Guinness Book of Records. They would be tasting a lot of hot peppers over the years!
- Your perception of saltiness and sweetness drops by around 30 percent at high altitude. This is one reason why airplane food doesn't taste great (even if it is high quality).
- The food industry does a lot of research into taste. One area is that of food and color. The results have been mixed because we all have individual food-colour associations. Most flavours are not associated with a color (lime and green is an exception). The researchers have found two general findings. The first is that the stronger the color-flavour association is, the greater the impact of color. And the second is that as color level increases, taste and flavour intensity increases. So the brighter the orange juice, the more the flavour.[7]

Taste
sense-ability

Here are some activities to get to know your sense of taste.

Good/ not-so-good things

Every sense has some things you will like about it and some you won't. Write them out here.

Good things about taste

Not-so-good things

How important is it?

On a scale of 1 to 10, how important is your sense of taste? Circle your answer.

1	2	3	4	5	6	7	8	9	10

Not important   Important

(?) What makes it important (or not)?

....
....
....
....
....

One day

Choose one day in the near future when you will be "taste aware."
Simply be aware of what you are tasting during the day. If you'd like, cut
out this form and carry it with you for the day.

Time	What am I tasting?	How does it affect me?

Taste test

Gather some "same size and shape" candies that come in a variety of
flavours (Life Savers® work well). They need to be the same shape and
size so you won't get a hint of what flavour it might be.

Close your eyes and plug your nose while a friend feeds you a candy
without telling you the flavour. Try to guess what flavor it is without
letting go of your nose. Continue to make observations for a minute or
so as the candy dissolves in your mouth.

Is there any change in the taste of the candy from the beginning to the
end of the experiment? Describe the flavors you experience.

Food and colour

Food and colour greatly influence each other (this is a good example of how the senses work together). For example, one experiment had people taste two glasses of the same white wine. The tasters described the two glasses as having very different flavours. How did this happen? The researchers had added red food colouring to one glass so the tasters thought they were tasting red wine.[21] What have you noticed about food and colour?

(?) **What are you favourite food colours?**

....
....
....
....

(?) **What food colours do you dislike?**

....
....
....
....

(?) **What have you noticed about your reaction to the color of foods?**

....
....
....
....

Sight

As you go through your day, you see many things, good and not-so-good:

A.M. As you wake up, you can see daylight peeking through the cracks in your curtains. You open them and sunlight streams in, creating patterns of light on your floor. You smile at yourself in the mirror as you get ready for the day. As you run to catch your bus, you see a car coming and hold back on crossing the street. Better to miss the bus than get run over. The sight of your bus going down the street leaves you peeved. When you get to work, you see everyone has gathered for a meeting you're late for. When you walk in everyone smiles and you feel relieved and welcomed.

P.M. You spend lunch in a nearby park and take the time to watch the birds and look at the flowers that are just starting to bloom. It relaxes you after your hectic morning. On returning to work, the pile of work on your desk doesn't look so large. On the bus ride home, you see an accident and feel upset because it looks like people got hurt. It's hard to get it out of your mind, so you go for a walk in the neighbourhood and look at your favourite houses. You see some neighbours and chat with them. When you return home, you watch some TV to relax and then head to bed.

4 sights

Before we move on to learn about your sense of sight, take a few minutes to think about sight. Write or draw four things you can see right now:

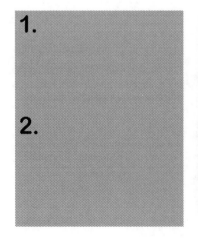

1.

2.

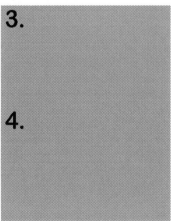

3.

4.

The Sensory Compounding Workbook

What is sight?

What you see are actually rays of light. Light is electromagnetic radiation that travels in waves. Light is emitted from the sun, light bulbs, stars and fire. Most of what we see is reflected light which is when light waves bounce off objects that don't emit their own light. Light has three parts: colour, saturation and brightness.

Why do we have sight?

Sight is the most developed sense in humans. Sight allows us to see. This sounds obvious, but we often take our sight for granted. You only have to walk around wearing a blindfold for a few minutes to be reminded how important sight is. Vision keeps us safe by allowing us to see danger. It also lets us see beauty. We can read and take in information using our sight. Sight lets us see movement, texture, color and shapes.

How sight works

Light rays enter the eye through the cornea, a protective film on the surface of your eye (sort of like a windshield). Then the light rays pass through the pupil (the black circle in the center of your eye). Your eye colour is the iris. It's a muscle that surrounds the pupil and changes its size. In low light, the iris makes the pupil bigger to let more light in and in bright light, it gets smaller to protect your eyes.

Just behind the pupil is the lens and it focuses the image onto the back surface of the eyeball, called the retina. The retina has millions of light receptors called rods and cones which send information to the brain by way of the optic nerve.

(i) When the eye sends an image to the brain, the image is upside down. It is the brain's job to turn the image right side up and then tell you what you are looking at. The brain does this in a specific place called the visual cortex.

Rods are long and narrow and identify shapes. They work best in dim light. There are more rods on the edges of the retina (or the "periphery"). Peripheral vision is when you look to the side of an object to better see it in low light. When walking a path in the dark, if you look to the side of the path, you will see better (this is a handy camping trick when you're trying to find the bathroom in the dark).

(i) Owls must have lots of rods! They can see a mouse moving over 150 feet away with light no brighter than a candle.[8]

Cones look like their name. They identify different wavelengths of light which the brain then processes into colour. You can't see colours well in low light because the cones don't work well in low light. They do best with lots of bright light.

The way in which light waves are translated to colour is really complicated. But we only have to look at a rainbow to understand color. A rainbow shows the spectrum of light that we are able to see. There are seven colors in a rainbow (red, orange, yellow, green, blue, indigo, and violet) and they are always in the same order. We are able to see so many colours beyond these seven colours because we can see mixtures of two or more colours. Artists spend a lot of time learning to mix colours to create the one they want.

Colour psychology

There are a lot of theories about the influence of colour on people but very little actual research using good scientific methods. Some beliefs about color date back a thousand years. We do know that color can impact your mood and behaviour, but this varies greatly between people, situations and cultures.

Warm and cool colours

The seven colors of the rainbow can be divided into warm (red, orange, yellow) and cool (green, blue, indigo, and violet) colours.
Warm colours can evoke feelings of excitement, energy, warmth and comfort, and sometimes aggression. Cool colors are thought to be calming, soothing, relaxing and can sometimes trigger feelings of sadness.

ⓘ All this talk about how color can affect you won't hold if you can't see colour. One in every twelve males and one in 200 women are color blind which means they cannot see one or more colours. The most common is red/green colour blindness, which means you can't see red, green or any colour that has red or green in it.

My preferences

Everyone has colour preferences. What are yours?

What are your favourite colours? What feelings/ mood do you associate with each of these colours?

What are your disliked colours? What feelings/ mood do you associate with each of these colours?

Seeing is believing - fun facts

- You blink every 2-10 seconds. Each blink lasts for a third of a second. This means your eyes are closed at least 30 minutes a day just from blinking.[8]
- Ever wonder why animals' eyes glow at night? It's because they have a mirror-like layer of tissue behind their retinas which helps them see better at night. When a light shines at the animal's eyes, they appear to glow due to the reflection.
- When paired with words, visual images help people learn faster and remember what they learned. So when you want to learn something, pair the words with some pictures.
- Companies spend a fortune on their logos. A good logo presents a picture that doesn't even need words. Starbucks dropped their name from their logo and Target needs no name after their logo! That is the power of visuals.

Sight sense-ability

Here are some activities to get to know your sense of sight.

Good/ not-so-good things

Every sense has some things you will like about it and some you won't. Write them out here.

Good things about sight	Not-so-good things

How important is it?

On a scale of 1 to 10, how important is your sense of sight? Circle your answer.

1	2	3	4	5	6	7	8	9	10

Not important   Important

(?) **What makes it important (or not)?**

....
....
....
....
....

One day

Choose one day in the near future when you will be "sight aware." Simply be aware of what you are seeing during the day. If you'd like, cut out this form and carry it with you for the day.

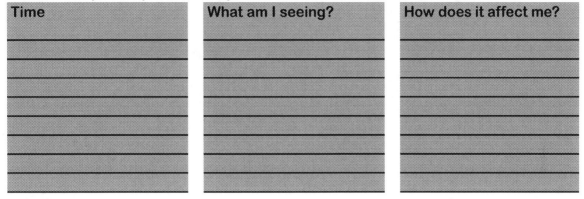

Time	What am I seeing?	How does it affect me?

Colouring books

Colouring is in and trendy right now and there are a lot of fun books available. What a great way to play with colour!

Develop an artist's eye

Betty Edwards has developed a method of learning to draw based on her observation that we can't draw because we can't *see*. So she teaches you to see and the result is you can draw! Her book is called *Drawing on the Right Side of the Brain*.

Beauty breaks

We often don't take time to "stop and smell the roses" (oops, that's another sense!). The visual equivalent is to take small breaks your day to look at something you find beautiful. It might be a rose. Or a picture, a person or an object. Make time for beauty.

Smell

As you go through your day, you smell many things, good and not-so-good:

A.M. The wonderful scent of coffee first thing in the morning (and more times through the day). The smell of burning toast tells you to unjam the toaster. The diesel from the bus nearly gags you, followed by a miserable ride in the elevator filled with way-too-much aftershave and perfume. Your workspace smells like the night shift's pizza and the flowers on your desk are still emitting a wonderful fragrance.

P.M. You go to lunch at a bakery café and nearly swoon at the smell of freshly baked bread. On the way back to work, you pass a garbage can that reeks and hold your breath so you don't have to smell it. When you get home, you can still smell the burnt toast so you light an incense stick with your favourite fragrance. You go to bed and breathe the comforting smell of your pillow and the faint smell of laundry detergent on your freshly changed sheets and thus soothed, fall asleep.

4 smells

Before we move on to learn about your sense of smell, start sniffing! Take a few minutes to take in your environment. Write or draw four odours you can smell (if you can't identify four, write as many as you can):

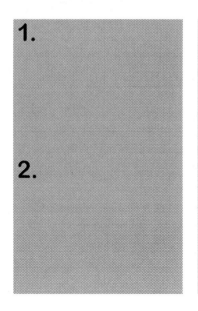

1.

2.

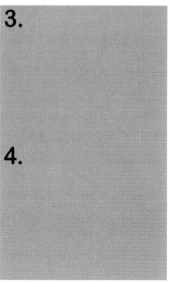

3.

4.

What is smell?

Smell is one of our two chemical senses (taste is the other). Odours are vapours which are tiny chemical molecules. Smell is unique among the senses in that it's directly wired into the brain. When odor molecules hit our sense receptors in the back of the nose, the smell signal is sent on an express route to the brain.

Types of smells

People can smell many different odours (some researchers estimate we can smell over 10,000). That's a lot to keep track of! To narrow it down, researchers create smell categories. The most common categories are camphor, musk, floral, peppermint, ether, pungent and putrid. Newer research classifies ten basic smells. Fortunately, all you need to know is what smells you like and don't like (and focus on getting more smells you like into your life).

My types

Write down your favourite and NOT favourite smells.

What are your favourite smells?

What smells do you dislike?

Why do we have smell?

Smell is protective

Odours can pack their bags and travel long distances. Smell is a long-distance warning device. Think of forest fire smoke or a coming storm, both can be miles away. Smell can also warn us from a lot closer—think of spoiled milk or rotten meat. So one of the functions of smell is to warn you of things that are probably not good for you.

> (i) You really can smell rain in the air or a storm coming. As the clouds roll in, they bring ozone, a form of oxygen. It is ozone that creates the fresh smell of coming rain.

Smell is directly wired to the brain—no long routes here! The smell nerves go directly to the part of the brain which deals with the association of emotions with memory. This wiring means we can't help the way we respond to some smells. Imagine opening a carton of spoiled milk and taking a sniff. Your face will scrunch up, you'll likely say "ew!" and you might feel the gag reflex. This makes smell a powerful survival mechanism.

Smell is emotional

There is some research that indicates we select our mates based on their smell. This is subconscious (at least most of the time!). Mothers can identify their newborns by smell alone within an hour after holding them![9]

Our emotional responses to smell are formed by association. Pleasant odours tend to create pleasant mood states while unpleasant odours lead to unpleasant moods. However, what is a pleasant smell to one person may not be to another. A good example is perfume—one person might love the smell and another might hate it.

> Anosmia sufferers [people who have lost their sense of smell] report feeling isolated and cut-off from the world around them, and experience a blunting of the emotions. Smell loss can affect one's ability to form and maintain close personal relationships and can lead to depression.[10]

Some researchers believe that the loss of an important memory gateway might be responsible for some of these symptoms.

Smell and memory

Smell and memory are closely linked. A smell can provoke a whole memory with all its emotions. This is involuntary (and due to the unique wiring of the smell system). Odour memory lasts a long time and outlasts memories from our other senses (for example, a visual memory or a touch memory).

If we smell something before or during a negative experience, that smell will be linked to that experience. The smell of wintergreen is rated as pleasant by Americans and really unpleasant in Britain where it was used in medicine and especially in analgesics in World War II.[11]

The good news is that unpleasant memories associated with a particular smell can be re-wired by new experiences. The unpleasant memory can be replaced with a more pleasant one.

Not all smell memories are negative. There are often positive memories associated with smells. There is even some research searching for ways to use the smell-memory link to enhance learning and develop treatments that can be triggered by smell.

> ⓘ One really interesting study used smell to regulate blood sugar! Insulin was injected into healthy male volunteers once a day for four days and their blood glucose was measured (it fell). At the same time, they were exposed to a smell. On the fifth day they were just given the smell, and, their blood glucose fell.[12]

Memories

What are some of your smell memories?

What smell makes you remember a positive experience? What was it?

What smell makes you remember a negative experience? What was it?

Smells fade

We quickly lose our ability to smell the same odour. Within minutes, you adapt to the smell (this is called habituation). It's why people can't smell themselves (like when wearing too much perfume or aftershave). If you light a scented candle, you won't be able to smell it after a while.
This likely serves a protection function. Our brains search for changes in our environment that might signal danger. Once you've decided this is a safe smell, the brain hunts for new smells that might signal something not-so-safe.

ⓘ Professional smellers use some tricks to "clear their noses." One is to leave the area and then return with a "fresh nose." If you want to know what your house smells like, leave it for a while and then return. Something about increasing your blood flow also seems to revive your sense of smell. Perfume testers run up and down stairs; you can run around in a room.

Smell and aging

As we get older our sense of smell declines. This also affects our sense of taste. 80% of people have some major smell dysfunction by the age of 80.

Good news

You don't have to wait for your sense of smell to fade away into the past. Brain scans of perfumers show that the parts of the brain that process smell get larger as they age. This might be the old adage "use it or lose it" in play. The more you actively work your sense of smell and seek out new smells, the better you can avoid the decline.

(?) How has your sense of smell changed over time?

....
....
....
....
....

The nose knows – fun facts

- You can't smell as well when lying down (researchers do not know why). So to really smell something, sit or stand up!
- Dogs and horses can smell fear in humans and humans might be able to as well. Some studies have found that humans can smell fear in the sweat of people who were exposed to scary things (like a horror movie or skydiving). We don't know much about this yet.
- The aboriginal people in Australia's Western Desert associate the smell of the rain with the color green. No wonder! The arrival of the annual rains transform the desert from a dry, dusty, parched landscape into a fragrant green paradise.[13] This is one example of how our senses work together—more on this later!

Smell sense-ability

Here are some activities to get to know your sense of smell.

Good/ not-so-good things

Every sense has some things you will like about it and some you won't. Write them out here.

Good things about smell	Not-so-good things

How important is it?

On a scale of 1 to 10, how important is your sense of smell? Circle your answer.

1	2	3	4	5	6	7	8	9	10

Not important   Important

(?) What makes it important (or not)?

....

....

....

....

....

One day

Choose one day in the near future when you will be "smell aware."
Simply be aware of what you are smelling during the day. If you'd like,
cut out this form and carry it with you for the day.

Time	What am I smelling?	How does it affect me?

Train your nose

You can increase your sense of smell by "training your nose." Wine
tasters and perfume testers do this for a living. You can start by simply
smelling things with more intention. Look up the seven smells and buy
some items for each smell. Match the smells to the category. Take a
wine course that teaches how to smell wine.

Create a smell map

A similar idea to the "One day" exercise was created by some
urban design researchers.[20] They had people walk around different
neighbourhoods and record what they smelled. Was it pleasant or not?
They then created a map to show the different smells in a city.

ⓘ The human nose is a powerful thing. The places where people recorded bad smells had more polluted air. Areas rated as having more pleasant smells had better air quality.

Why not walk your neighbourhood? The researchers developed a great colour-coded tool called the Urban Smellscape Aroma Wheel. You can use this tool as you walk your neighbourhood to identify the smells you experience.

You can download a pdf version of it at: www.researchswinger.org/smellymaps/urban_smellwheel.pdf

Touch

As you go through your day, you touch many things, good and not-so-good:

A.M. You shiver as your feet hit the cold floor when you reluctantly get up. You enjoy the warmth of your coffee cup in your hands as you wait for your place to heat up. You always enjoy your morning shower as the hot water flowing over your skin gently wakes you up. You step outside into a cold morning and feel your face tingle and your lungs contract. When you get to work, you sit in your chair and feel its welcome support on your lower back as you settle in for the day.

P.M. You start to get a headache and massage your temples which helps. A co-worker comes in and tells you she got engaged and you hug her which feels great. On your way home you get pelted by wind-driven snow and it hurts. You change into your flannel pajamas that feel so soft on your skin. Your cat climbs into your lap and you feel her soft fur on your hands and the vibration of her purring on your legs. More flannel as you climb into bed, and surrounded by softness and warmth, you drift off to sleep.

4 touch things

Before we move on to learn about your sense of touch, start touching! Take a few minutes to think about touch right now. Write or draw four things you are touching (if you can't identify four things, write as many as you can):

1.

2.

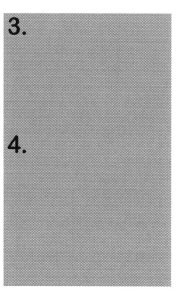

3.

4.

What is touch?

Touch is the least studied of the senses, yet it's an essential sense. The first sense to develop in a human fetus is touch. Without touch, we could not survive. We would have trouble walking, we wouldn't know where our body parts are, nor could we react to burns, cuts or other painful events.

Touch lets us feel temperature, both hot and cold. It also plays a huge role in our sense of where our bodies are in space (called proprioception). It allows us to feel texture, smoothness and a huge variety of other touch information.

How touch works

The skin is the touch organ and it's the largest organ we have. Our skin protects our internal body parts from the outside world. Skin is made of layers of cells, nerves, sweat and oil glands, hair follicles—and touch receptors.

The skin has many touch receptors that send messages to the brain via the spinal cord. There are three types of receptors:

Thermal receptors detect temperature, both heat and cold.

Pain receptors detect fatigue or tissue destruction. Pain is also activated by extreme heat or cold. Pain can trigger a reflex action, like when you pull your hand away from a hot stove.

Mechanical receptors sense motion, both external (at the surface of the body, e.g. the feel of your feet on sand) and internal (the position of your body in space and deep tissue sensations called proprioception).

> ⓘ Have you ever had repeated ankle sprains? It is now thought that the reason for this is that the proprioception sense is damaged along with your ankle ligaments. When we lose the ability to know where our ankle is in space, it's easier to turn over on it again. So the prescription to prevent more ankle sprains is lots of balancing exercises which work to restore proprioception.

Touch and emotion

We've been talking about the physical sense of touch which includes temperature, pressure, pain and texture. Another important part of touch is emotional. Touch signals also go to the emotional and social centres of the brain.

Our physical experience of touch is influenced by our emotions and the context in which touch happens. For example, a hug from our partner is likely to feel great where the same hug from someone we don't like will feel very different. That same hug might feel different if we're angry at our partner. Same touch, different feelings!

Humans need affectionate (good) touch, especially when young.

(i) It's long been known that children raised in orphanages sometimes develop "failure to thrive syndrome." They do not develop normally and often die, even with adequate food and medical care. What's missing is touch. The children were not held, cuddled, rocked or soothed with a gentle touch.

There is strong evidence that a lack of affectionate touch causes depression, violence, memory deficits, and illness.[14] We don't know why something as simple as touch can affect your body so greatly. Leading theories speculate that lack of touch interferes with attachment and creates high stress.

On the other hand, affectionate touch can make us feel good, decrease stress, decrease recovery time from injuries and illness, and improve our thinking.[14] Massage therapy is gaining popularity as an effective treatment for a variety of physical problems (or just because it feels good!).

(?) **What types of touch feel good to you?**

....
....
....
....

(?) **When has touch triggered an emotion for you?**

....
....
....
....

Touch points - fun facts

- Players on sports teams that have lots of celebratory touch tend to perform better. [15]
- One reason that elderly people are at risk of falls is because they get less touch information from the soles of their feet. Walking barefoot can help.
- Expert readers of Braille report that they interpret the touch sensations automatically (without any conscious effort) the same way expert readers of written words convert them into sounds without any conscious effort. The motor cortex of the brain changes in response to Braille reading, with areas devoted to touch sensations from fingertips growing larger. [16]
- The sensations of tickle and itch are closely related to touch and pain.
- Bats fly with breathtaking precision because their wings are equipped with highly sensitive touch sensors that respond to even slight changes in airflow. [17]

Touch sense-ability

Here are some activities to get to know your sense of touch.

Good/ not-so-good things

Every sense has some things you will like about it and some you won't. Write them out here.

Good things about touch	Not-so-good things

How important is it?

On a scale of 1 to 10, how important is your sense of touch? Circle your answer.

1	2	3	4	5	6	7	8	9	10

Not important   Important

(?) **What makes it important (or not)?**

....
....
....
....
....

One day

Choose one day in the near future when you will be "touch aware."
Simply be aware of what you are touching during the day. If you'd like,
cut out this form and carry it with you for the day.

Time	What am I touching?	How does it affect me?

Feel your environment

Walk around your home and touch things. For each object, run
your fingers over the surface and note what it feels like. What is the
temperature? Is it light or heavy? Rough or smooth? If it's a shirt or
other clothing item, press it to your face and note the sensations.

Sensory Compounding

If you've worked through this workbook, you'll have become more aware of the impact your senses have on your well-being. Our quality of life is greatly influenced by our senses and we can influence how our senses affect us. That's what Sensory Compounding is all about.

Sense-ability

Sensory Compounding teaches you to become more aware and intentional about your senses and to use all five senses together to create inner calm and peace—anywhere, anytime. This sense-ability can help you reprogram old, unhelpful reactions and create new helpful, relaxing reactions to sensory information.

Conditioning and learning

Sensory Compounding is based on conditioning theory. Conditioning means learning. You learn to use all five senses to trigger peaceful and calm reactions.

Conditioning is when we learn to associate a sense with an event, person, place, etc. If it's a happy association, when we experience the sense, we will experience a positive reaction. If it's a negative association, we will experience a negative reaction.

> (i) For example, some people find the smell of turkey triggers happy memories and a feeling of happiness. Others may associate it with being ill and feel fearful and worried (if they got food poisoning by eating turkey). Still others may feel sad because they associate the smell of turkey with a family breakup that happened at Christmas.

Sometimes, we are aware of these associations. And sometimes we aren't. A big part of recovering from trauma is learning what sensory triggers are associated with the trauma and then reprogramming them so they don't trigger traumatic reactions. It's common for a person to be unaware of some triggers for trauma.

Sensory Compounding can help you learn new responses to established sensory triggers. You can also just learn new ways to use your senses to trigger pleasant responses such as calmness, peace and relaxation.

Compounding

There are many methods out there to use one sense to create a positive response. Aromatherapy is one, art therapy is another. What makes Sensory Compounding unique is that you combine all your senses to create a powerful stimulus for relaxation or inner peace.

How does it work?

Sensory Compounding works by pairing sensory cues (called Sensory Stimulating Elements) to the desired response of relaxation and peace. There are two phases to Sensory Compounding.

Phase 1

This phase consists of the guided visualization experience. Identify one of your favorite safe place guided visualizations and find a comfortable space to listen to this visualization. Remember to tune into your five senses to create a complete sensory experience of peace and relaxation.

Phase 2

In this phase, we use Sensory Stimulating Elements to stimulate the desired response. You learn to pair the Sensory Stimulating Elements with a safe, peaceful place during the guided visualization.
This phase is also where you strengthen the associations you made during the visualization and introduce the Sensory Stimulating Elements. The Sensory Stimulating Elements will become your cues for your peaceful, calm relaxed state. Once they are "programmed," you can use the elements to create the feelings of your safe, peaceful place—anywhere, anytime.

A safe place in your home

You can create a safe place in your home, a haven for you to relax in. People get quite creative with this! Here's some ideas:

 One woman's safe place was on a beach, so she created a beach in her home. She put up posters of beach scenes and plays recordings of waves and other beach sounds. She puts her favourite suntan lotion on (she loves the smell of it). She makes herself a margarita before lying in the hammock under a heat lamp that feels like the sun.

Another person does relaxation before sleep, so he added his safe place to his bedside table. He placed a picture of the mountains (his safe place). A pine cone which still smells like trees also serves as his touch point with its textured surfaces. He plays the sounds of wind in the trees on his clock radio speakers. His toothpaste flavour reminds him of the crisp mountain air.

A travel kit

It's great to be able to take your safe place on the road so you can relax anywhere. You can choose Sensory Stimulating Elements that are easily carried with you. Here's an example:

After a hard day's work, you feel stressed out and angry as you ride the bus home. So you use your Sensory Stimulating Elements travel kit to reach your calm peaceful place. You pop a lemon flavoured candy into your mouth and the taste reminds you of your safe place. You put your headphones on and play the music you chose while looking at the picture of your safe place on your phone. You rub your fingers over the pebbled surface of your aromatherapy diffuser locket while breathing in the scent of your safe place. By using all five sensory cues, you feel your body relax as tension leaves your muscles and your mood lightens and calms.

It takes practice

Sensory Compounding is a learning process. It can take some practice to reach your calm and relaxed state as a response to your Sensory Stimulating Elements. Each person has their own path and the time it takes varies. There is a progress review at the end of this section that can help you monitor how you're doing.

Phase 1 activities

Once you have completed the guided visualization, complete the following activities. This helps to strengthen your experience of your safe and peaceful place.

What was the sensory experience?

Describe your calm, peaceful safe place in detail.
Where was it? Who was with you or were you alone? What were you doing? What were the feelings you experienced?

Describe
each sense

Describe each sense that was present in your safe place. This information will be used when you choose your Sensory Stimulating Elements so include as much detail as you can.

Hearing

Did you hear birds singing? Did you hear music? If so, what were you hearing? What other sounds were there?

Taste

Were you eating anything? Or drinking something? What food was present? Were you chewing gum or a candy? Could you taste the air?

Sight

What did you see? What colours were strongest? What textures were there? Was it bright or darker?

Smell

What did you smell? What did the air smell like? Was there water? Was there food present and what did it smell like? Were you wearing a fragrance?

Touch

What were you touching? What was touching you? Did you feel the wind blowing? Did you feel the sun on your skin? What was the temperature like? Was it cold, warm or hot?

My safe place

On the following page, create a picture of your safe place using these hints. Making a picture of your safe place strengthens your memory of it and you can use it as one of your Sensory Stimulating Elements.
You can really let loose and get creative! Here's some ideas:

 You can use the following page or go bigger. You can get larger paper or an art board to use instead.

 Draw or paint your safe place. Use colours and textures. It doesn't have to be a perfect masterpiece, it just needs to symbolize your safe place.

 If you don't like drawing, try collage. Get some magazines and cut out pictures that fit for you. Glue them onto this page.

 Some people go 3D and make a collection of objects. They can be in a bowl, glued together into a sculpture, whatever fits for you!

 You can add an aroma if you want to add another sense.

When you have finished, cut this picture out and place it somewhere you can see it. You could take a picture of it and keep it on your phone so you have it with you.
Make sure you choose a safe place to put your picture of your safe place!
It will remind you that you have this safe, special and calm place.

My safe place

The Sensory Compounding Workbook

Phase 2 activities

Once you have completed your picture of your safe place you can now add the Sensory Stimulating Elements. The Sensory Stimulating Elements will become your cues for your peaceful, calm, relaxed state.

Adding the elements

Think of the senses you experienced in your safe place visualization and match them to Sensory Stimulating Elements. Some Sensory Stimulating Elements that people have used include:

Hearing
- music or soothing sounds on your phone or stereo
- wind chimes

Taste
- gum, candy, mints
- tropical drink

Sight
- field of daisies
- a picture of your safe place

Smell
- scented candles, diffusers, perfumes
- peppermint

Touch
- an old comfortable shirt
- a soft blanket.

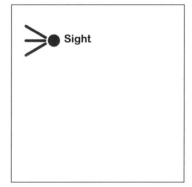

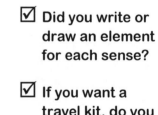

☑ **Did you write or draw an element for each sense?**

☑ **If you want a travel kit, do you have portable elements?**

Rating your progress

It can take some time and practice to reach your calm and relaxed state as a response to your Sensory Stimulating Elements. Each person has their own path and the time it takes varies.

On a scale of 1 to 10, how well are you doing in being able to use your Sensory Stimulating Elements to cue your relaxed, peaceful response? Circle your answer.

1	2	3	4	5	6	7	8	9	10

Not working at all   **Can consistently
                                                            relax on cue**

Improving your sense-ability

If you aren't where you'd like to be yet, here are some things that might be holding you back. For each one that you rate as "needing more work," write out how you can strengthen your ability. You can revisit this checklist again until your sense-ability is where you want it.

☑

If you aren't used to working with your senses, you might need to spend some more time on getting to know them. Try reviewing the workbook and re-doing the activities (you did do them, right??). If you didn't, it's a good idea to complete the activities so they strengthen your sensory awareness.

☐ **I did this well**

☐ **Needs work**

(?) **What do I need to do?**

....
....
....
....

☑

Have you engaged all of your senses? Do you have Sensory Stimulating Elements for all five senses? If not, go back and create some for the missing senses. See the worksheet on page 49.

☐ I did this well

☐ Needs work

(?) What do I need to do?

....
....
....
....

☑

If you are using your Sensory Stimulating Elements and they do not produce a relaxed, calm state, you might need to repeat the visualization recording again. As you do, imagine your elements as you experience your safe place. Some people need to repeat this several times.

☐ I did this well

☐ Needs work

(?) What do I need to do?

....
....
....
....

☑

What was the environment like where you tried to relax? Was it a crowded environment with lots of noise and stimulation? Consider trying it at home first where you can control the environment. As you get better at your response, gradually try it in more challenging environments.

☐ I did this well

☐ Needs work

(?) **What do I need to do?**

....
....
....
....

☑

Did you complete the picture of your safe place? If not, revisit pages 47-48 of this workbook. This is an essential step that strengthens your memory of your safe place.

☐ I did this well

☐ Needs work

(?) **What do I need to do?**

....
....
....
....

Best wishes

By completing the activities in this workbook, and practicing until you can consistently activate your safe, relaxed place on cue, you've added a powerful tool for your well-being.
I wish you all the best as you find your path to peace and calm in this challenging and ever changing world we live in.

April Nelson

References

1. "Exploring the Sense of Hearing." Fractal Enlightenment. Accessed January 8, 2016. http://fractalenlightenment.com/ 31260/life/ exploring-the-sense-of-hearing.

2. "Hearing for Communication (and Interaction)." Accessed January 8, 2016. http://www.audira.org.uk/en/modernising-attitudes-to-hearing-care/ item/19-hearing-for-communication-and-interaction.

3. Zampini M and Spence C. (2004). The Role Of Auditory Cues in Modulating The Perceived Crispness And Staleness Of Potato Chips. *Journal of Sensory Studies,* 19: 347–363.

4. "Taste, Our Body's Gustatory Gatekeeper." Accessed January 7, 2016. http://www.dana.org/Cerebrum/2005/ Taste,_Our_Body%E2%80%99s_ Gustatory_Gatekeeper/.

5. Griffioen-Roose S, Hogenkamp PS, Mars M, Finlayson G & de Graaf C. (2012). Taste of a 24-h diet and its effect on subsequent food preferences and satiety. *Appetite,* 59(1):1-8.

6. Citron FMM, Goldberg AE. (2014). Metaphorical Sentences Are More Emotionally Engaging than Their Literal Counterparts. *Journal of Cognitive Neuroscience,* 26(11): 2585-2595.

7. "Taste and Smell." Accessed January 7, 2016. http://www.tastingscience. info/explained/Sensory.htm.

8. "Your Sense of Sight." Accessed January 8, 2016. http://hes.ucfsd.org/ gclaypo/senses/download/sight.ww/thinkquest.html.

9. Kaitz M, Good A, Rokem AM, Eidelman AI. (1987). Mothers learn to recognise the smell of their own infant within 2 days. *Dev Psychobiol.* Nov;20(6):587-91.

10. "Psychology and Smell - Fifth Sense." Accessed January 7, 2016. http:// www.fifthsense.org.uk/what_is_smell/psychology/.

11. Herz, RS. (2005). Odor-associative learning and emotion: Effects on perception and behavior. *Chemical Senses,* 30, i250-i251.

12. Stockhorst U, Gritzmann E, Klopp K et al. (1999). Classical conditioning of insulin effects in healthy humans. *Psychosomatic Medicine,* 61: 424–35.

13. "Storm Scents: It's True, You Can Smell Oncoming Summer Rain - Scientific American." Accessed January 7, 2016. http://www. scientificamerican.com/article/storm-scents-smell-rain/.

14. "The Sense of Touch and How It Affects Development | Serendip Studio." Accessed January 11, 2016. http://serendip.brynmawr.edu/exchange/ node/4356.

15. "How Our Sense Of Touch Affects Everything We Do." The Huffington Post. Accessed January 11, 2016. http://www.huffingtonpost. com/2015/01/20/neuroscience-touch_n_6489050.html.

16. "The Cutaneous Sense (Touch) | in Chapter 04: Senses | from Psychology: An Introduction by Russ Dewey." Accessed January 11, 2016. http://www. intropsych.com/ ch04_senses/cutaneous_sense.html.

17. "Keen Sense of Touch Allows Bats to Fly with Breathtaking Precision." The Hub. Accessed January 11, 2016. http://hub.jhu.edu/2015/04/30/ bat-agility-flight-sensors.8.

18. "How Hearing Works." Accessed January 8, 2016. http://www. hearingfoundation.ca/how-hearing-works/.
19. "Designing For All Five Senses." Accessed January 2, 2016. http://www. fastcodesign.com/3050854/designing-for-all-five-senses.
20. Quercia D, Schifanella R, Aiello LM, McLean K. (2015). Smelly Maps: The Digital Life of Urban Smellscapes. In *Proceedings of the 9th International AAAI Conference on Web and Social Media* (ICWSM).
21. Morrot G, Brochet F, Dubourdieu D. (2015). The Color of Odors. *Brain and Language*, 79:2, 309-20.

About the Author

April Nelson is a Canadian Author and Registered Psychologist who has a private therapy practice in Edmonton Alberta, Canada. She has a passion for helping others and the Sensory Compounding Workbook is a result of her vision to provide individuals with a alternative healing tool.

Printed in the United States
By Bookmasters